NAP·SNACK·WIN!

OFFICE CAT INC.

HOW TO
GET AHEAD
IN BUSINESS
WITH OFFICE CAT

A MEOWNAGEMENT GUIDE
TO PURRFESSIONAL SUCCESS

Ariana Klepac
& Pete Smith

Smith
Street
Books

CONTENTS

MY STORY

People always ask me, 'How did you get so successful?'.
I might be a billion-shrimp mog-nate these days, but it's
all thanks to my grandfather, Freddy. He started life as a
stray kitten never knowing where his next meal was coming
from, but ended his days a highly respected business leader
and billionaire. He learned everything he knew not from
going to college, but through the 'school of life'.

When Freddy was a kitten he used to hang around the local
fishmongers every day, watching the produce being unloaded
and delivered. He sniffed every box of crustacea and fish
carefully and followed closely behind in case anything
dropped to the floor. If he meowed and looked extra-cute
the delivery driver would throw him a pilchard or two.

My grandfather listened to the fishmonger wax lyrical
about shrimp for hours: which were the best; which were to
be avoided; which looked promising but were all shell and
no meat. This is where Freddy learned how to strive for the
very best and accept nothing less.

In return for the food and tuition, my grandfather chased
the mice, rats and pigeons out of the shop, which of course

Freddy became so knowledgeable about fish and crustacea that he was choppered in to nearby fishing ports for his advice on the day's catch.

he enjoyed. This is where he first discovered the concept that work can and should be 'fun' - a maxim that has been passed down to me.

The fishmonger came to dote on Freddy. He had all the fish he wanted and gradually did less and less work in return. The fishmonger bought him fluffy rugs and soft cushions to knead and lie on, and he ended up sleeping most of the day. He became quite a drawcard for the shop and customers flocked to see the gorgeous fluffy cat. The fishmonger continued to prosper until he owned not one but many shops. He always thought of my grandfather as his lucky charm and, on the fishmonger's death, Freddy was his sole beneficiary. With his new-found wealth my grandfather started up Office Cat Inc. The company was passed down from father to son and so to me.

Since I was a kitten I have observed the symbiotic relationship between humans and cats, and eventually came to the conclusion that the secret of feline success lies in sticking close to our human friends. I can honestly say that without the assistance of humans (together with my remarkable personal charm and good looks), I wouldn't be where I am today. After many requests, I have written this book to set down a few of my business secrets to help other aspiring fluffy entrepreneurs fulfil their dreams. There are also plenty of useful notes for humans who would like to help and support them to accomplish their goals.

Office Cat Inc. is an umbrella company for a variety of businesses: importing and exporting (mainly shrimp), freshwater and deep-sea fishing, and cardboard box manufacturing.

PART ONE

SO YOU WANT TO BE A SUCCESS?

Top 6

OFFICE CAT'S TIPS FOR BUSINESS

1. DON'T BE A WORKAHOLIC: It's important to have some quality time for yourself. I mean, what's all the gruelling delegating between naps for if you can't find time for yourself to do the things you want?

2. NETWORK, NETWORK, NETWORK: At least several times a day you should wander up and down the street and the nearest alleyways to make important new connections and grow business.

3. WORK FROM BED: Influenced by another leading furry global business guru, who likes to work from a hammock on his private island, I like to spend days at home strategising in my velvet leopard-print igloo.

4. GET OFF THE TV: When you're at home, stop wasting time sitting on the TV and go out into the world. There are so many fascinating things to sniff and scratch. You never know where you might find inspurration - it could be lurking by the nearest garbage bin.

5. THE IMPORTANCE OF LISTENING: If you listen you will hear things that are to your advantage. When I was still just a kitten I developed an uncanny ability to hear sounds that indicated things were going to go my way, such as the sound of a refrigerator door opening.

6. FOLLOW YOUR DREAMS: My dreams are usually about shrimp and tuna, so that's what I focus on whenever I need motivation. I have recently commissioned a new water feature for the lobby at Office Cat Inc., featuring a rampant shrimp and tuna, to remind us what we're all working for.

THE FUR FACTOR

"Once you have the Fur Factor,
all miracles are possible."

TIDDLES T. RUMP

There are many furred animals in this world, from the
fawning dog to the clumsy bear, but having the Fur Factor
is something quite different. It is a quality exclusive
to the cat family. No matter whether you are a mighty lion
prowling an African savannah, or a ragdoll cat on a velvet
cushion in New York sleeping off a bowl of smoked salmon,
all cats have it to some degree.

From ancient times, cats have been revered as a 'higher
species', worshipped for their intelligence, beauty and
exemplary level of personal cleanliness. Yes, dogs have
also been popular and some misguided individuals have
deified them too, but cats are undoubtedly more popular.
Basically it's the same principle that applies to love -
no-one wants something that can be obtained with no effort.
The highest prize is hard to get. And that is exactly what
cats are - we're a challenge. But we're worth it.

MY INSPURRATIONS

All the great business minds have role models, and here are a few of mine to motivate you to greatness. After reading this, make a list of all the cats who have influenced you.

TOMMASO ASSUNTA: Tommaso, like my grandfather Freddy, went from being a stray kitten to the beneficiary of a huge estate. He inherited $13 million dollars from his Italian owner, Maria Assunta. Like my grandfather, he invested his money in a business run with the assistance of human support staff. Wise cat.

UNSINKABLE SAM: This marvellous mouser, originally known as Oscar, was a German ship's cat who allegedly sailed on the ill-fated vessels the 'Bismarck', the 'Cossack' and the 'Ark Royal'. All three ships were sunk but, each time, Oscar was rescued and therefore eventually earned the nickname 'Unsinkable Sam'. He left the navy and retired to Northern Ireland to see out the rest of his days on dry land. His purrsistence and courage are an inspurration to me.

CATMANDO: Joint leader of the Official Monster Raving Loony Party in Britain (with his owner Howling Laud Hope), Catmando was a hero to all purrlitically minded moggies. Following the death of the legendary head of this party in 1999, Screaming Lord Sutch, Catmando and Howling Laud Hope tied for first place in the vote for a new leader. After Catmando's tragic death caused by traffic accident in 2002, the OMRLP put forward a proposition that there should be cat crossings for all major roads. A tragic end for a promising purrlitical strategist.

STUBBS: Honorary Mayor of the historical district of Talkeetna in Alaska since 1997, Stubbs has put his town on the map and tourism has risen exponentially. Allegedly, Stubbs patronises the local restaurant each day, to mix with his fellow townsfolk. His drink of choice is a wineglass of water spiced with some catnip. Following suit, I like to trot down to the local milkbar on the corner every day, where a bowl of lactose-free milk is waiting for me - in return I attract attention from cat-loving walk-ins who become dedicated return customers. It's good to feel like you're in touch with the common folk.

MARU: This pioneer of internet marketing, a Scottish Fold, rose to fame in his homeland of Japan. He has a strong sense of branding in that his signature is his love of cardboard boxes - well, any boxes really. Maru's video feed is the seventh most popular channel in Japan. I have great plans for the internet too, which I will discuss later in the book.

GRUMPY CAT: Enough said. This beautiful creature (real name 'Tardar Sauce') shot to fame in 2012 all because of her charming underbite. Her business sense and strong grasp of personal branding are second to none.

Finally, I would like to pay tribute to some other cats who have changed history. If it weren't for the following cats, our world might be a very different place: 'Macak', the close friend and brilliant assistant of scientist Nikola Tesla; 'Nothing', the existentially challenged cat of Jean-Paul Sartre; 'Jellylorum', the cat belonging to British poet T. S. Eliot, and the inspurration for the musical 'Cats' (incidentally, I have several composers currently vying for the position of writer of my upcoming musical, 'Fur!'); and finally President Abraham Lincoln's White House Cat Team, 'Tabby' and 'Dixie'. It is well known that Dixie ran the country for a while after the untimely assassination of the president.

Of course, one of my other great inspurrations is the global business genius Richcat Branson. From him I have learned to nap in my hammock on my private island Catuai, rather than in the office. I get a lot more high-quality sleeping done there.

THE PURRER

To make a good impression in business, you need to travel
in a style that befits your status. For road travel I have
an official Office Cat Inc. limousine (affectionately known
as the 'Purrer'). I also like to take it when I have to visit
the vet so when I arrive in all my glory, the vet instantly
knows that I'm not to be messed with, nor mercilessly poked
and prodded in my hind-quarter area.

Top 10

OFFICE CAT'S KEYS TO SUCCESS

1. BE A DREAMER NOT A DOER: There are plenty of humans out there who can do stuff for you. You just need to brief them clearly so you can go back to sleep.

2. LEARN FROM YOUR MISTAKES: Once, my personal chef gave me a smaller portion than normal for breakfast. I didn't complain as I wasn't particularly hungry that day and therefore the same small portions started appearing at every meal. I learned to complain even if I didn't really want or need more food.

3. NEVER GIVE UP: Humans give up too readily. But when cats need something they never give up. Rather, they will accelerate the pressure until they get what they require. For example, if I want food I tend to hang around the kitchen looking cute. If this doesn't work, I utter a gentle meow. The following stages are jumping up on the kitchen bench, knocking things on the floor and, sadly, the final stage is reverting to nips and light scratches. Purr-sistance pays.

4. REMAIN IN YOUR COMFORT ZONE: I mean, if you're not lying on a comfortable carpet, an old cardigan or a squishy couch how are you expected to work?

5. YOUR GOALS SHOULD NOT BE MONEY-BASED: Money is pretty useless to cats, so think in terms of crustacea, canned foods or treat packets.

6. TIMING IS EVERYTHING: Whether you are trying to catch a fly or get to the communal feed bowl before your colleagues, make sure you get in first.

7. GO WITH YOUR GUT: If it tastes good, eat it. If it doesn't, throw it up.

8. DON'T BE ASHAMED OF YOUR CHARISMA: I was born charming. I can't help it. It has opened doors for me (mainly refrigerator doors) and I'm not afraid to be proud of it.

9. CONCENTRATE ON GETTING TO THE TOP: Whether it's the kitchen bench, a tree or the head of a large corporation like Office Cat Inc., never take your eye off the prize.

10. STAY FOCUSED: Luckily this is easy for cats. Some of the greatest furry business leaders can concentrate on a scuff mark on a wall for many hours at a time.

PART TWO

HOW TO GET PEOPLE UNDER YOUR PAW (AND KEEP THEM THERE)

USE YOUR CUTES

"Forget smarts, use your CUTES to win friends
and influence people. Work cute not smart."

HENRY FURRED

It's remarkable how little effort it takes to wrap humans around your paw. I find that the slightest movement or noise I make sets humans off squawking with delight.

When the Human Support Staff are particularly mutinous, the merest glimpse of my belly fur works wonders. If that doesn't do the trick, I begin an ear-cleaning session. This tends to have a hypnotic effect on the humans and can calm even the most incendiary of situations.

Other weapons in my arsenal of cute are my adorable 'fluffy ginger jodhpurs' (or hind legs as viewed from behind), my glorious fluffy white tail and my four oversized, white velveteen paws. Of course, like any supermodel, it takes a lot of work to look this good and I spend a huge part of each day grooming and fluffing out my cattributes. Before events I get my personal groomer to brush my fur to a high shine.

COMMUNICATION

"Of all our myriad ways of communicating,
chin-tickling is still the most universally
effective language."

ALBERT MEOWNSTEIN

Good business communication can mean the difference
between success and failure. Fortunately, I have no
problems in this area. I am a master linguist and speak many
cat languages, including Siamese, Burmese and Tonkinese.
I am still on a personal journey to understand Humanese,
which is so unnecessarily complex it could take all of my
nine lifetimes to master. However, I am proficient enough
to run a company that employs a large Human Support Staff
and we have learned to understand each other.

The Fluffy Meownagement Team and I have the attitude that
any lack of comprehension between the humans and us is
'their' problem, not ours. The communication skills of the
cat are clear and concise, while humans have an unfortunate
tendency towards verbosity and over-complication in all
their workplace dealings. As many business leaders will
tell you, it's best to keep it simple. The feline vocabulary

of 100 vocalisations is more than enough. Therefore, I have developed my Triple-S rule for the humans: Simplify, Shorten and Summarise. However, I welcome any patting, scratching or tickling to emphasise key points, and there is no time limit for that.

Despite the distinctions between cat and human languages, there are some noises we have in common. The fact that they convey something very different in each language can cause problems though. Therefore, we have asked the humans to avoid two noises. The first is the hand clap. Although this is apparently a sign of appreciation from humans, it means 'skedaddle' to a cat, so all forms of applause or spontaneous claps of delight are banned. The second is the yowl. In a female cat it signifies a special happy feeling. However, when a human yowls, they are usually in extreme pain.

For any direct verbal communication coming from a human staff member, the Fluffy Meownagement Team have recording devices that they can switch on should the human's talking continue for longer than 2 minutes. The human is encouraged to keep speaking into the device for as long as they like and the cat will listen to the rest at their leisure.

There are various telecommunication systems used in business, from the telephone to Facetiming and Skype. I prefer face-to-face communication as without the aid of body language and facial expressions, I am often misunderstood.

I use my bluetooth headset not for making calls, but for listening to live feeds from the fishing port about the quality of the day's shrimp haul.

THE GINGER FURY

It's important to have a sense of style wherever you are,
even in the air. The decor inside my personal Office Cat
Inc. jet, the 'Ginger Fury', is cat-friendly and opulent.
There are squishy couches and shagpile mats everywhere and
there is a solid 22-carat gold, constantly dripping tap
in the bathroom area, which also features self-cleaning
marble litterboxes. David Attenborough's 'The Life of
Birds' is on repeat on huge screens throughout

the jet. Food is provided by my personal three-hatted chef, whose knowledge of crustacean-based cuisine is second to none. There is a luggage area under the plane, in which Human Support Staff can also be transported in appropriate crates when required – although we kindly offer sedation to make the journey less stressful.

BODY LANGUAGE

"Studying ear position
is one of the most vital ways of reading
a person's state of mind."

SIGMUND FURRED

When you are communicating with someone, it's not just what you say that counts. Our bodies have their own non-verbal language, which can give away important information – this can obviously have ramifications on business dealings.
To be an effective communicator you need to know how to read body language and know how to use your own body and four legs to make the right impression. I usually start communicating with clients long before I open my mouth.

POSTURE: Luckily, for the most part, the same rules apply for humans and cats. If a cat or a human

I have a lovely smile, which encourages people to approach me. But it can quickly turn to teeth should the need arise.

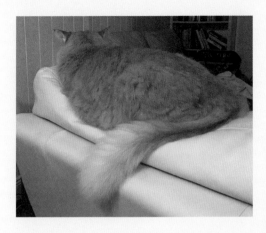

Here I am exhibiting possibly one of the most unmistakeable of all cat body-language postures. It signifies that without the speedy appearance of some kind of edible peace offering, you've lost me and my business.

has their back or shoulders hunched and their fur is standing on end, you can tell something is wrong. However, one important difference is if a fluffy staff member falls over and rolls onto their back, this is considered an extreme display of joy; but if a member of the Human Support Staff does this, it's usually time to call the emergency services.

PAWSHAKE: Again, human business leaders have been making a big mistake with their ridiculous meet-and-greet pawshakes. As anyone knows, it is one of the greatest of insults for a human to even try to touch a cat's paw, let alone grasp it firmly and then shake it ruthlessly for several seconds. Cats see this as a minor act of war and I have sadly seen many such encounters end in claws.

EYE CONTACT: Humans have been getting this wrong for centuries. Some well-meaning

This is another of my friendly body postures, which clearly says to the human staff 'please approach and pat at will'.

foolish human once suggested that you should maintain eye contact during meetings. I've seen pitiful humans with their eyes red and watering profusely, attempting a crazed stare for hours during meetings. This causes a high level of stress and discomfort for the fluffy staff, so at Office Cat Inc. there is a ban on continued open-eye contact between humans and cats. We encourage our humans to carry out a slow blink every three seconds.

TEETH: When a cat shows its teeth, it's pretty obvious what that means - even to a human. However, humans continue to go around with stupid smiles on their faces, imprudently displaying as many teeth as possible. We have had to invoke the 'Toothless Smile Rule' for humans when in the vicinity of a fluffy staff member.

TAILS: The evolution of humans over the millennia has sadly resulted in the loss of their tails. I feel sorry for them, as you can say so much with a tail. Regarding my fluffy staff, I look for employees who trot around with their tail up. Cats with attractive tails love to show them off. I was born lucky and have an adorable fluffy white tail. I have a signature move, known as the 'Fizzy Tail', which I use to show extreme appreciation or enthusiasm.

EAR POSITION: This is a constant source of confusion for fluffy members of staff when dealing with humans. All cats can read each other by looking at the ears: forward means playful; up means alert; back means overstimulated, irritated or defensive; and back and flat against the head means trouble with a capital T. The problem is that humans prefer to keep their ears constantly back and flat against their heads, so this makes the cats perpetually agitated when talking to them. As a result, we tend to prefer to employ human staff whose ears naturally stick out - the further the better. Hairnets and snoods are encouraged for female human staff and the new fashion for man buns has been a Garfield-send for human ear-reading purposes.

If I am unceremoniously woken from a deep sleep by a thoughtless human staff member, I tend to adopt this body language, which clearly says 'approach at own risk'.

THE ART OF NEGOTIATION

"The inimitable negotiation skills of the cat
are mainly due to its inherent lack of comprehension
of the words NO, DON'T or CAN'T."

WHISKERS CHURCHILL

When it comes to getting what you want or closing a deal,
as well as razor-sharp claws it's vital to have razor-
sharp negotiating skills. My cute and fluffy exterior
hides a determined and sometimes ruthless interior.
However, when negotiating it's always best to stay calm
and put your point across without stooping to hissing,
biting or clawing.

The days of the 'pawshake' deal are long gone. These days
it's vital to get a pawprint on contract. If I'm negotiating
with a human I show my approval with an increased volume of
purring or by doing a few figure-eights between their legs.
If things aren't going my way I just start to clean my
private parts or, if things really get heated, I might
throw up a furball - this clearly means that I'm no longer

interested in negotiating and please leave. However, when I roll over on the desk and expose my belly for tickling, it means the deal is closed.

I tend to capitulate more readily with human clients and prospective suppliers if they adopt the age-old ritual of bringing a gift, preferably edible. Catnip-infused gifts, although fun, often seem to end in the human negotiator ending up with the better deal, and tend to create a miasma of confusion for myself and other fluffy negotiators, so it's best to be wary of these.

However, I am not ashamed to say that I do have a couple of lucky charms of my own that I employ when meeting a human for an important negotiation. Try these out to give your cat-human negotiation success a boost. First, don't rush to empty the ensuite litterbox. This may ensure the other party chooses to agree to your terms in a hurry rather than remain in the prevailing atmosphere.

Second, if one of your fluffy staff happens to have brought you a 'gift' in the form of a mouse or bird, place it on the desk between you and the human, as this also tends to bring the deal quickly to a close in your favour. (I've heard that some humans use a rabbit's foot in a similar way.)

I'm not the only one with tricks up my sleeve. When a human I am negotiating with brings a brush out of their briefcase, I know it's a lost cause and I will give in to their demands.

PART THREE

PURR-SONNEL

THE IMPORTANCE OF GOOD STAFF

"The only things that can't be delegated
are napping and using the litterbox."

GEORGE W. BUSHYTAIL

A company is only as good as its staff and it pays to
have a good purr-sonnel meownager whose job it is to seek
out the very best. Regarding the Fluffy Meownagement Team,
I prefer experienced staff, and I usually find my best

performers from the local cat shelters.
That said, kittens tend to bring a
great energy and I know both the cats
and the humans seem more engaged when
a new kitten joins the team.

Of course, when it comes to fluffy
staff, excellent candidates will
often randomly wander in off the
street and then it's just a matter
of offering them a hearty bowl of

sardines and hoping they'll become permanent fixtures. Our purr-sonnel meownager simply does a quick scan of their resume (flea, worm and other feline ailment vaccinations).

The part-time option is extremely popular with cats, and many choose to split their time between different companies. As long as there's no major conflict of interest, I am happy with that.

When looking for Human Support Staff, it's obviously unnecessary to say that can-opening skills are a top priority. A background in fishing is also desirable. (I also hold bi-weekly, four-hour can-opening workshops for the humans to hone their skills and keep them abreast

of any new techniques or innovations in can-opener design.) As well as providing food for the fluffy staff, humans can take care of things like production, furrnance, marketing, sales and office administration. Always delegate the small stuff like this.

HIERARCHY

"Humans are important but cats
are more important."

GEORGE PAW-WELL

It might be fashionable in this day and age to make the
hierarchy in a company appear as invisible, or 'flat',
as possible. However, when it comes to a company made up
of both cats and humans, it's simply a ridiculous notion.
Cats are born leaders. We are commanding, invoke worship
in humans and, for thousands of years, the human race has
been completely comfortable with cats being in charge.
In fact humans seem at their happiest when taking orders
from cats - there's nothing they won't do for us. Humans
know their place in the scheme of things.

Humans are larger and therefore built for physical work
and menial jobs - you could say they are the 'cart horses'
of Office Cat Inc. Cats are small and agile and highly
intelligent. We are also far more personable and hygienic.
Therefore, we are best suited to meownagement roles.

At Office Cat Inc. every department is headed up by a fluffy meownager. Then there is a 'pool' of humans whose mission is to do whatever, whenever, and basically to keep the company ticking over during meownagement nap-time and see to all the fluffy needs of the company.

OFFICE CAT INC. COMPANY STRUCTURE

CEO, OFFICE CAT

FLUFFY MEOWNAGEMENT TEAM

POOL OF HUMAN SUPPORT STAFF

JOB INTERVIEWS

"Talent will get you in the door,
but belly rubbing
will keep you in the room."
CHAIRMAN MEOW

No matter which side of the desk you're on, interviews are
a constant source of stress to workers everywhere. In
primitive, human-only companies, interviews are based on
applicants preparing, and then employers subsequently
poring over, pages of meaningless qualifications, followed
by a monotonous verbal exchange of personal histories
in a call-and-response format. However, at Office Cat Inc.
I have developed my own, more dynamic interview style.

INTERVIEWING CATS

Hearing tests are carried out at all prospective fluffy
staff interviews. A sense of smell
is important and we ask prospective
employees if they can identify the
subspecies of a catnip plant. We
require that the applicant can
hear the noise of a refrigerator

door being opened, or a spoon tapped
on a metal can, from a distance of 500
metres. We prefer fluffy employees
who are able to distinguish between
the sound of a cat treat packet being
rustled and the sound of a human
potato chip packet. Extra points are
given for a correct estimate of the
amount of treats left in the packet to

the nearest gram. Finally, if the furry interviewee
is aware of the latest share prices on shrimp, tuna
or sardines, that's a bonus.

INTERVIEWING HUMANS

During any human interview, a fluffy staff member will
produce a furball on demand, and I watch and analyse the
human interviewee's response. If there is any wrinkling
of the nose or vocalisations that suggest disgust, I know
the person won't be a 'good fit'. However, if the human
immediately expresses concern and runs to find a cloth,
bingo, we know we've found our new employee.

STOPWATCH TEST: We also conduct a
few 'Stopwatch Tests'. The first one
is the Litterbox Stopwatch Test. The
interviewee is asked to empty and refill
a used litterbox. Points are deducted
for any face-pulling or hesitation.

CAN-OPENING TEST: The second is a simple can-opening test. Interviewees are required to open cans using three different types of openers. There is also the 'improvisation test' where the human is asked to try and find a way to open a can should the hideous situation ever arise where no can-opener is available when a fluffy staff member needs a meal.

OBSTACLE COURSE: Heavy-footed human staff who willfully clomp about, not watching where they're going, are a hazard at Office Cat Inc. We prefer light-footed humans who keep their eyes glued to the floor at all times with no thought to their own safety. Therefore, during interviews we have set up a 'test course' where prospective employees are asked to walk up and down a passageway. We note if they watch the floor to avoid the fake paws and tails that we have sticking out from under cupboards along the walk. A buzzer sounds if contact is made. They also walk past an empty treats bowl with a full treats packet glaringly obvious above it on the shelf. If they are thoughtless enough to not refill the bowl on their way past, points are deducted.

PATTING TEST: The penultimate stage of the interview process is the Patting Test. The interviewee is required to carry out a 10-minute pat, scratch and tickle session with me. I look for the hallmarks of a good staff member: one who remembers to scratch the top of my head, behind my ears, rub my belly (but not for too long), and avoids the paws and legs. Special points are given for humans confident enough to rub my cheekbones and get in behind my whiskers.

BRUSHING AND COLLAR-REMOVAL TEST: Finally, there is the brushing and collar-removal test. When brushing, does the human lavish extra attention on the top of the cat's head and give the required and respectful 'wide berth' to the

backside area? (We take pleasure in grooming that ourselves.) Can the human take off and replace a cat's collar without causing distress? As everyone knows, there is a 10-second 'window' and then the cat is gone and the collar stays off.

INTRODUCING A NEW STAFF MEMBER

"If there's no need for the first-aid kit
after introducing a new staff member,
you've probably chosen well."

HENRY HISSINGER

During the interview process it's important to keep in mind
how the prospective staff member might fit in with the rest
of the company. It's no good hiring someone with excellent
skills if they will never be able to be in the same room as
another staff member without baring their teeth and making
unpleasant high-pitched noises or, conversely, whimpering
and retreating behind a filing cabinet.

Bringing a new fluffy
member of staff into the
fold is a delicate matter.
It's easiest to employ cats
that have been brought up
in multi-cat households, as
they are quicker to mix and

make friends. But to be safe, we generally have a quarantine area where new fluffy employees go for a day or so to 'acclimatise'. Then for a succession of days we have a 'meet and greet' session with one fluffy employee at a time. It's usual for there to be a bit of initial bickering, but if the negativity continues through the probation period, we have no choice but to un-hire the troublemaker.

When we hire a new human staff member at Office Cat Inc., we find they are generally easy to introduce into the company. They mostly get on with other humans and it's rare that they resort to biting and scratching. They usually can't wait to get to know the fluffy members of staff. We have a special induction ceremony where a new human staff member is granted a 30-minute 'get to know you' window with each individual fluffy staff member, which includes an offering of treats and a pleasant scratch-and-pat session, where the cat will brief the human on their favourite forms of patting and their individual culinary preferences.

1. Highly valued

2. Need to cut back

3. Unfortunately...

4. Sorry to lose you

5. Good luck!

NATIONAL
CASSETTE TAPE RECORDER

RECORD   REWIND   FF   PLAY   STOP

MONITOR   REMOTE   MIC

THE PROXY

Of course it's vital these days to provide the personal
touch in business, but there are just some things that
are simply a waste of a meownager's time and expertise;
for example, matters such as signing off on the yearly
profit and loss statement or staging a hostile takeover
of a competing company.

One of my most valuable staff members answers only to me.
He is my personal assistant and is known around the place
as 'The Proxy'. He's my Can-Do Man, my aide-de-camp, my
'2OC'. He handles things for me when I am too busy to deal.

The Proxy never wavers from his instructions and I can
always trust him to do a good job. He never complains
and no burden is too heavy for him.

For textbook situations, such as having to retrench
a long-term member of staff due to cost-cutting measures,
I leave it to The Proxy. He has a recording device set
up with a numbered series of buttons. Each button plays
a recorded message from me with suitable comments and
sentiments. It's an efficient process.

MEETINGS

"If an argument goes not in the direction
of your choosing, the best course of
action is to throw up."

ANCIENT SIAMESE PROVERB

Meetings with the Human Support Staff are a necessary
evil. Humans seem to thrive on them. It's a time when
they can hold court and feel they have a say in office
proceedings and the direction of the business. Of course
they don't, but I like to keep them happy.

Meetings are a good opportunity to reassert yourself as
the charismatic leader and to ensure you keep staff under
your spell. Like famous leaders of the past I always arrive
late to create a sense of healthy agitation and expectancy.

I like to start a meeting with a summing up of the previous
one. I ask one of the keen Human Support Staff to do this.
They love to keep extensive miniutes anyway, so I ask that
they include lots of detail to give the fluffy staff enough
time to wake from their naps. A long summary at the end of a
meeting is also desirable for the return of sleep. Once the

floor is mine, I like to start with a joke to lighten the mood. A favourite is my 'Two Irish dogs go into a cafe...'

As leader, it's best to guide rather than dominate the meeting. Really, there's no need to talk at all if you'd rather not, as the humans are more than willing to do it all. The occasional tail twitch is enough to show your approval or to signal a change of topic. If you're too busy to attend the meeting, you could simply Skype from home. Or better yet, a still image of yourself on a screen can be enough to make your presence felt and inspire your staff. When a human brings up a difficult topic, such as the age-old question of why can-opening workshops are necessary,

a good tactic is to quickly tip the wink to one of your furry colleagues to sprawl in the middle of the boardroom table, bearing his fluffy belly. The humans immediately squeal with delight and line up for tummy rubs, the subject of workshops wiped from their brains.

Place a time limit on each topic. One to two minutes is adequate, unless of course the topic is shrimp or tuna.

One of the most annoying things about meetings with humans is their tiresome preference for cats to keep their eyes open while humans are talking (especially as they like the meetings to take place during daylight hours).

As anyone who knows anything about good business practice understands, this is just not possible, but they won't listen to reason. Therefore, to remedy the situation I have

To deal with the human staff's insistence on cats keeping their eyes open while humans are talking, I developed the Eyes Wide Shut method of sleeping with the eyes open (patent pending).

been holding secret after-hours training sessions with the fluffy staff to perfect the Eyes Wide Shut (EWS) technique of sleeping with the eyes open, developed by me. This has saved the day and now the humans can drone on while we blissfully clock up more valuable hours of sleep.

Many prototype methods of dealing with the humans' Eyes Wide Open policy were trialled. Some were not successful.

Checklist

MEETING INNOVATIONS

Be innovative with your meetings. Set an inspiring
theme or combine the meeting with a fun activity.
Here are some great ideas:

✓ Remove all chairs from the meeting room so everyone
  has to stand up - except the cats, of course, who are
  happy to lie on the floor or desk. When the humans
  have to stand, they tend to abbreviate their
  monologues and rants.

✓ Combine the meeting with a fun shrimp-shelling workshop.

✓ Hold the meeting at the local fishmarket.

✓ Prepare the meeting room with essential oil burners.
  Catnip is good, but the effects on the Fluffy
  Meownagement Team can be unpredictable.

✓ Encourage Human Support Staff to translate all
  mention of profits or percentages in terms of shrimp
  or tuna to keep the fluffy participants engaged.

✓ Similar to a drum circle, try a belly-rubbing circle.

✓ Never allow a human to bring in a laser pointer to draw attention to a projected diagram. Trust me, all hell will ensue.

✓ Staring contests between humans and cats can often decide a sensitive argument. The cat will always win.

✓ To indicate that you would like the human to stop speaking, commence cleaning your private parts.

✓ If a meeting gets out of order, ask a Siamese member of staff to let out one of their legendary, ear-splitting yowls.

✓ Ensure human staff never use the phrase 'pass a motion' in a meeting as it can be misinterpreted by fluffy staff members.

GROOMING AND DRESS CODE

"There's nothing more likely to inspire confidence than the sight of a freshly groomed tail."

MEOWILYN MONROE

As we all know, you don't get to the top of the corporate cat tree without perfect grooming! I expect my Fluffy Meownagement Team to be well groomed at all times, wearing smart collars (bells optional). Collars can only have one bell as 'double-belling' can become quite cacophanous. Monthly belly and butt clips are recommended. Humans are encouraged to wear comfortable clothing – that

I have quite an extensive wardrobe of collars and ties – one to suit every occasion. My favourite designers are Gianni Furrsace, Stella McCatney and Georgio Purrmani.

is, clothing which is deemed comfortable by the fluffy staff when sitting on human laps. We ask that humans wear soft (or, better yet, no) shoes around the office so there are no accidents with unwary paws or tails.

There has been a complete ban on faux fur for the humans as it can be distracting and confusing for the fluffy meownagement. One staff member convinced himself he was in love with a fluffy clutch purse belonging to one of the heedless humans. It led to a serious disruption in my fluffy staff member's productivity and state of mind. The clutch purse was fairly unrecognisable after said staff member had completed his full courting ritual.

TIMEKEEPING AND LEAVE

"Work is the thief of naps."

FRANCIS BACON-BITS

There are some mundane housekeeping issues that are important, such as timekeeping. A caring boss will also have a flexible policy towards leave. Office Cat Inc. timesheets strictly require a full 8 hours of work to be completed each day by the Human Support Staff. Equally, the fluffy staff are bound to complete 18 hours of full sleep - napping not included. If this is not followed to the letter, the meownagement will lose concentration and the business (and office chairs and carpets) will suffer. Office Cat Inc.

All fluffy staff are offered counselling after gruelling shifts of 20 minutes or longer. We try to avoid burnout.

Fluffy staff, myself included, are encouraged to take a nap whenever and wherever.

has a huge advantage over other companies as it runs 24-7. This is vital for the fluffy meownagement to be able to achieve their sleep quota. They tend to be more dedicated than the human staff and are happy to work all hours - they don't shoot out the door at 5.30 pm on the dot.

When it comes to leave, it's important to put staff wellbeing first. Humans get the usual amount of sick days per year, and the cats get the usual amount of sick hours per day. Additional compassionate fluffy leave is offered at peak furball times, and 'special leave' can be granted for female cats at those sensitive times of year.

STAFF PROBLEMS

"Social media addictions to Furrbook and Litter
are the enemy of workplace productivity."

ARIANNA FLUFFINGTON

Of course you will have troubles with staff now and then,
and it's important to deal with issues fairly but firmly.
The following are some of the most problematic concerns.

CATNIP ABUSE: First, there is the serious topic of substance
abuse. While humans might occasionally exhibit problems
with alcoholic beverages, some fluffy members of staff have
been known to succumb to the siren song of recreational
stimulants. I sadly had to let one staff member go as his
experimentation with Extreme Catnip in business hours got
out of hand and it was impossible for us to get any sense out
of him. (I feel certain that this must be where the origin
of the word 'catatonic' lies.)

INTERNET ABUSE: The internet has been a boon to the modern business human and cat. However, there are always going to be some staff who abuse it, by constant use of things like Furrbook and

'Prawn porn' is one of the more unpleasant staff issues we have to deal with.

Litter. Many a time have I walked past an unknowing member of staff who has been conducting an on-screen love affair during office hours. If fluffy staff are found with 'prawn porn' (salacious shelled shrimp images) on their computers, they risk instant dismissal.

AGGRESSIVE BEHAVIOUR: All antisocial behaviour should be discouraged. It came to my attention at one stage that one of the younger, more feisty members of the fluffy staff had organised a secret Catfight Club on Friday nights in the knitting room. I obviously put an immediate stop to this.

BREEDISM: There is a zero tolerance policy against breedism and discrimination at Office Cat Inc. We are an inclusive company and welcome all breeds of cats, including the often overlooked Abergavenny Apathetic and Omanian Overgroomer.

PART FOUR

HIGH FURRNANCE (AND OTHER MINOR MATTERS)

PROFIT AND LOSS

"Never have times been so difficult for cats
since the Great Shrimp Shortage of 1933."

MEOWGARET SCRATCHER

Furrnance is a boring yet necessary topic that I feel
requires at least a brief mention. Luckily for me I started
out with a small loan of a million dollars from my father,
but after that it was up to me to grow my business and
personal wealth. I have always tried not to worry too much
about costings, and I generally never get any accountants
in before starting a new business venture. If I think it's
good, it IS good. I adhere to the old adage 'Build it and
they will come'.

It is increasingly difficult in this world to make a profit
and especially so since the Global Furrnancial Crisis. But
luckily the popularity of cats is on the rise and Office Cat
Inc. has this phenomenon on its side.

When it comes to accounting, I have to say that I've never
been a numbers cat. I have a feline form of dyslexia, which

I believe is common with a lot of other high-fliers in the world of business. However, I'm street-wise and shrimp-smart and that's all that matters. Also, when looking at a wad of cash, I immediately know what it translates to in terms of shrimp, chicken or cat treats. I can calculate down to the nearest milligram.

However, profitability can be a burden and it's important to take measures. Tax is a constant issue. Luckily there are many personal expenses that I can claim. But, if the situation worsens I may have to decamp to my private island in the Pacific, Catuai.

And if - Garfield forbid - I fall on hard times, I do have a rainy day fund. I have 20 containers of frozen shrimp meat, which I have exported to a refrigeration plant in the Cayman Islands.

For complex calculations I have developed my own adding machine, the 'Shrimpulator'. I have done away with meaningless numbers on the keys and replaced them with pictures of shrimp.

BRANDING

"Whether it's on a hot air balloon,
on the back end of a bus, or on the handle of a
litter scooper, get your brand out there!"
DON DRAPURR

Branding is so important in the modern world. You have to
stand out from the crowd – just as I do on a personal level
whenever I walk down the street. Over the years the Office
Cat brand has achieved global recognition, so I thought it
only fair to share a few of my secrets with you.

First you need to work out what your brand is. When I
orignally thought about the Office Cat Inc. brand, I looked
in the mirror and asked myself, 'What am I? What is my
brand?' Basically it's cute, it's fluffy, it's commanding
and it's ginger. Then I asked myself, 'What's important to
me?' That's easy – eating and sleeping and getting whatever
I want, whenever I want, with the least amount of effort.
That's how I came up with the Office Cat Inc. motto.
Although I considered 'Success Through Sloth', I decided on
'Nap. Snack. Win!' It says it all, really. And of course
what better image for the logo than my own cute ginger face?

THE OFFICE CAT SIGNATURE COLLECTION

As I am the face of my brand, and my face is so handsome and popular, it made sense to create The Office Cat Signature Collection for other cats in business who aspire to my personal style. It's a high-end line including collars (both formal and informal), bow ties, personal tags in silver and gold (diamonds optional), Murano glass food bowls, Carrara marble litterboxes and platinum-backed grooming brushes.

I have also brought out a bottled spring water product called 'H$_2$OC', which we serve in our offices globally.

More recently I have been approached by a Parisian company to market my own scent - LITERALLY my own scent, called 'Chat de Bureau'. The cologne will include base notes of mullet and top notes of catnip.

One of my lovely Human Support Staff used to make a delicious shrimp, carrot and brown rice dish for me at home every night. She was single and childless so I know it was probably a joy to do this, rather than a chore, and the experience enriched her life. Each day I would eat the delicious concoction and the fluffy staff would always beg for some. So I asked the human staff member if she could make enough for the whole Fluffy Meownagement Team. So she went from making one portion to ten per day. I realised we could be onto something, and maybe we could 'go commercial'. She would do anything to please me so she got a couple of friends involved and we started to market the product under the banner of 'Office Cat's Shrimp Delight'. Unfortunately the human couldn't keep up with the demand so I thought it would be easiest if I just got the recipe from her and organised things myself. She was happy with her generous one per cent share of profits and has continued to create new recipes for the product line, 'Office Cat's Crustacean Collection', which became such a successful business that it was eventually floated on the stock exchange.

I like to know that while I'm busy napping, people will be seeing the Office Cat Inc. brand float by their home on my branded hot air balloons.

One day soon Office Cat Inc. will expand into space. I've already sent a probe, Shrimpseeker 1, to search for potentially crustacean-rich planets.

OPERATION OFFICE GALACTICAT

Of course my biggest dream is to conquer territories slightly further away. Everyone's heard of Laika the dog who went into space, but not many have heard of Felicette, the French cat who was rocket-launched into space in 1963, then safely parachuted back to earth. Although it's quite hush-hush at the moment, I have a team of aerospace engineers working on Operation Office Galacticat. I mean, the writing's on the wall. Those shrimp in the ocean aren't going to last forever!

GET YOUR FACE OUT THERE

Like other fluffy business billionaires, I am a purrfect
example of a leader who is as famous as their own brand.
My face is my fortune and I make sure that I plaster it on
any surface where as many people as possible will see it.
Billboards on busy highways are ideal and my cuteness
stops traffic. I am currently investigating having my
face carved on a nearby mountain, along with the faces
of Garfield, Sylvester and Felix. I am also going to be
featured on the cover of the next issue of 'Mewsweek'.

NETWORKING

"The most important business contact
of your life could be sniffing around
the nearest garbage bin."

POOPERT FURRDOCH

I cannot stress the importance of this topic for both humans
and cats alike. Luckily cats are masters at this. You will
often see a cat disappear out the door at the crack of noon
to carry out a full day of networking, and they won't return
until late at night. You never know where you could meet
your next important contact: perhaps in the muddy drain on
the corner or on the abandoned mattress up the back lane.

The best contacts
are local contacts,
so I tell my reps
that it's a good idea
to get to know your
local territory well.

Find a good spot on the street
and lounge nonchalantly. Try not
to look too desperate.

You can't beat the tried and true methods of networking, such as tree-top lookouts and ambush points.

Not everyone will be accessible at all times, so you need to go looking at random times of day. If no one is around, you can always leave a 'wee-mail' in a well-frequented place for potential new fluffy business partners to find.

There are two types of networking. One is the fluffy kind and one is the human kind. As I've already discussed, the human is an easy target and will always be very eager to hear what you've got to say. They may well invite you home and then extend an open invitation to visit whenever you like. With any luck you can develop a wide network of these humans in your area.

Networking with other cats is not for the faint-hearted. Most cats prefer to network only with family or extended family. However, occasionally I'll come across a real fluffy charmer whose friendliness and powers of persuasion know no bounds. (I'm not ashamed to say I'm a bit like this myself.) One can usually tell quite quickly if you are going to be well received. If backs are arched and hideous noises emitted, it's best to make a hasty and respectful exit. It's their loss.

STAYING RELEVANT

"The future of cats is in the internet."

Boo-Boo Gates

If you don't keep up with scientific knowledge and the ever-changing methods of doing business, you'll be left behind. You have to move with the times and it pays to be an early adopter of new technologies.

As already discussed, the internet has proved a Garfield-send for cat-based business around the globe, originally spearheaded by the powerful Lolcats campaign. Therefore, it's critical to know how to take advantage of this medium.

All the top business leaders of the world have an internet presence. I am constantly encouraging my fluffy meownagement team to create embarrassing videos of themselves to upload to our Chewtube channel, as this brings in new business without fail.

We have a stunt cat coordinator who comes in to assist, and we have hired directors Steven Spielfur and Francis Furred Cattola to add a purrfessional touch.

Social media is a great way of networking, as well as advertising and creating sales. Furrbook is possibly the most important of these media, but there's also Litter, Whiskergram and Patchat. Finterest can also be quite useful for creating seafood-based vision boards when working on a new project.

We do have an external software development department, whose job it is to create apps for the feline global community. Currently our top technocat, Mark Zuckerfurr, is working on a new food-selection app called 'Nom or Not' where suppliers can submit photographs of potential new food products for cats. The cat can simply hit one of two keys with their paw, 'Nom' or 'Not', thereby providing the suppliers with instant valuable market research.

Another app in development is one concerned with safety in the feline community. It provides a map showing the nearest cat-friendly safe house in the area. The maps also note areas to avoid, where there are properties with unsecured dogs.

OFFICE EQUIPMENT

"Humans are like monkeys.
Through play they find amazing
uses for office equipment."

DAVID CATTENBOROUGH

In order to do a good job, your workers must have good tools. Office Cat Inc. has very particular needs when it comes to office equipment due to the company being 50 per cent fluffy. There is a distinct lack of 'paw-operated' machinery in this world (which is why it's vital to have Human Support Staff with opposable thumbs).

I've seen humans experiment and find all sorts of amusing uses for some items. For instance, keyboards - those wonderfully comfortable daybeds - have been adapted by our clever humans for typing up correspondence. One human staff member also discovered that our stapler pillows were filled with little bits of metal that could be pushed through sheets of paper to keep them together. We encourage this kind of 'play' for our humans at all times as it's both adorable to watch and often useful. Following is some general advice on the kinds of equipment to have around.

You can never have enough packaging materials. Empty boxes, shredded paper and bubble wrap are always in high demand, especially as the humans are always wasting it to wrap and send parcels.

Trackpads are preferable for humans' computers as The Mouse can prove distracting for fluffy team members.

Calculators with numbers are meaningless. However, 'shrimpulators' with symbols for shrimp on each key, instead of numbers, make sense and provide motivation when it comes to doing sums. 50 dollars means nothing, but 50 shrimp...

It was a great day when the new slimline, extended keyboards were invented. I remember the old days of chunky keyboards when that annoying square bracket key would get stuck in my ear.

Finding the right paper stock is vital.
I like to personally test any new sample
by attempting a four-hour nap on it. My
favourite is catte art 140 gsm.

As well as being able to print out interminable
office documents, printers must be comfortable and
large enough for a fluffy member of staff to be able to
stretch out full-length. They need to be able to withstand
repeated jumping on
and off.

There should be a
deliberate lack of
filing cabinets, as
piles of paperwork
are to be encouraged.
They are comfortable
to nap on.

The human staff are
always trying to
bring in pot plants,
but we have had a lot
of 'accidents' with

I like to test all the office equipment
myself. This printer has withstood
my vigorous '21-jump test'.

these, as the fluffy staff tend to view them as restroom alternatives. Instead, we have had to bring in the hydroponic-only rule for plants.

Finally, don't forget to buy a couple of those 'pens' that the humans are always bleating about. However, watch out as they are very territorial about their pens. They can become quite aggressive and the only situation I can liken it to is a dog growling while it guards its bone.

Backlogs of paperwork have traditionally been frowned on in many workplaces. However, at Office Cat Inc. they are encouraged as they are extremely cosy for fluffy staff.

THE 5 HABITS
OF HIGHLY EFFECTIVE CATS

1. Napping

2. Grazing

3. Flexibility

4. Immaculate grooming

5. Balance

OFFICE SECURITY

"The most important thing is
knowing how to get your shrimp.
The second is knowing how to protect it."

AL CATONE

Security is a high priority at Office Cat Inc. Kai, our
SWAT-team trained member of the Fluffy Meownagement Team,
is stationed on the roof of Office Cat Inc. 24-7. Special
tuna, shrimp and sardine sensors have been fitted near the
front door. With Kai coming from a Siamese background, he
doubles as the building alarm as well.

We do a lot of job rotation
at Office Cat Inc. and
all try our paws at the
various roles. The on-
roof security job is one
that is quite popular
among the fluffy staff,
including myself.

Rottweilers may boast about being the
best door security, but I can be just as
formidable when roused.

Here I am demonstrating rooftop surveillance to my staff. Um... I think we'll need to put in a call to the fire department to get me down again.

There's a fantastic view from the roof of the office, its environs and any half-empty bowls of food that might be on offer in the vicinity.

For dealing with sensitive documents (such as the monthly Chicken Chews invoice) we have a full-time paper shredder by the name of Sox. When we advertised for this position we were inundated and received applications from more than 20,000 furry hopefuls.

However, Sox was the lucky winner as he confined his shredding to the designated documents and did not stray into the human staff bathrooms and cause havoc with their toilet paper supplies.

PART
FIVE

SHRIMP, SHRIMP, SHRIMP! WORK SHOULD BE FUN

OFFICE DESIGN

"Mats, mats, mats.
You can never have enough of them ."
MACATMA GANDHI

The architecture and interior design of the workplace has
a huge bearing on staff wellbeing and productivity. Happy
staff tend to work 'better' (we don't like to say 'harder'
these days) and this results in a corresponding upturn
in profits.

Office design has gone through something of a revolution
in recent years and it's obvious that cats have been the
influence here. Thanks to other global corporate giants,
the boring cubicle-style office has gone out of fashion
and has been replaced with the
modern cat in mind - large open areas
connected by climbing frames and
ladders, with lots of cosy couches
and large windows that provide
plenty of sun-spots on the floor
to bask in.

Multi-platform work stations are good
as long as the staff sharing them get on well.

Office Cat Inc. has become a world leader in ergonomic work station design. Unlike human-only companies, who are so territorial about their desks and chairs, we encourage 'hot desking' as well as 'hot chairing' - my own innovation where anyone can use any work station they choose at any time in any way they please (on, under, behind or inside).

NOT ALL IDEAS ARE GOOD IDEAS

A catnip maze was an innovation that seemed a good idea at the time, but we lost several members of the Fluffy Meownagement Team for two days and had to send in a search party armed with smoked salmon to lure them out.

The humans suggested using small, foot-powered scooters to get around the office. But the potential damage to tails and paws was too dire to contemplate. Instead, small round robotic vacuum cleaners were employed to float around the floor and are a fun way to get around (they also double as cleaning equipment). Unfortunately they only seem to suit the feline staff.

When it comes to originality in use of office furniture, I don't think anyone is quite as creative as me.

Checklist

OFFICE INNOVATIONS

✓ Ban doors that close. We are trying to introduce open-plan bathrooms, although the humans don't seem to be on board with this particular innovation and need further convincing.

✓ Forget the stairs: rope ladder bridges are the new thing. If they are skinny and rickety and take everyone an age to cross, requiring the assistance of another member of staff, all the better, as this brings cats and humans together. Every trip to another floor becomes a team-building exercise.

✓ Strategic Thinking Domes are also a useful addition to the office and are perfect for quiet study and top-line problem-solving.

I get some of my best work done in my Strategic Thinking Dome. When I am in here I am not to be disturbed for ANYTHING – unless of course it is to ask me what I would like for lunch.

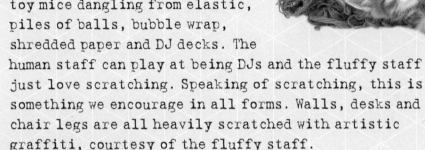

✓ 'Play areas' are the latest thing in office design. Innovate with toy mice dangling from elastic, piles of balls, bubble wrap, shredded paper and DJ decks. The human staff can play at being DJs and the fluffy staff just love scratching. Speaking of scratching, this is something we encourage in all forms. Walls, desks and chair legs are all heavily scratched with artistic graffiti, courtesy of the fluffy staff.

I like to practise post-nap yoga at my desk. It works well for clearing the mind and sharpening the appetite.

✓ Include recreation rooms that suit both the cats and humans. Ping-pong tables are good as the humans enjoy the game and when a ball hits the floor, the cats become engaged. Similarly, knitting, yoga and tai chi rooms work well.

✓ Groovy 'shrimp bars' and Sylvester- and Garfield-themed conversation areas are perfect for chilling out. After all, us mog-nates don't want to be known as tyrants. Stock up on turkey liver dental treats to encourage furball removal. You might find the humans prefer to chill at their desks.

MY OWN PRIVATE ISLAND

Due to my unprecedented success, I was fortunate enough
to purchase my own private island in the Pacific called
Catuai. It's a beautiful place teeming with birdlife and
slow-moving rodents, and I love to spend as much time there
as possible, dozing in a hammock or up a tree. We hold our
yearly conference there and the staff, both feline and
human, love it. To avoid a formal meeting situation,
I like to fly clients and suppliers there, so we can relax
and get to know each other. After we arrive on my private
jet, the 'Ginger Fury', guests are greeted with a shrimp
cocktail complete with a tuna jerky swizzle stick and
a catnip lei. As well as being a delightful retreat from
the hubbub of city napping, one day I might move there
permanently, should my tax situation become unmanageable.

ENCOURAGE CREATIVITY

"Forget thinking outside the box.
Think INSIDE the box."

CATFUCIUS

I love to encourage creativity and am generally in agreement with the other business experts out there about

how best to achieve this. Following are some of the most effective methods that I have used at Office Cat Inc.

1. BLUESKYING: This is a particular favourite with the fluffy meownagement. It involves going outside and lying on the ground and looking up at the sky for inspurration. The humans are slightly resistant and waste most of the time fussing around with

sunscreen, hats and sunglasses. Often blueskying can lead on to the next method.

2. CREATIVE NAPPING: Human business leaders only seem to have recently cottoned on to the benefits of napping and daydreaming, but we cats have been practising this method of creative thinking for millennia. If time spent napping is a measure of creativity, my meownagement team are definitely up there with Meowchelangelo and Shakespurr.

Predictably, most of the fluffy staff's suggestions tend to be shrimp- or seafood-based.

3. CATERAL THINKING: This is similar to lateral thinking, but it involves coming up with solutions that require the least amount of effort.

4. EXPLORE DIFFERENT CULTURES: Once a month we have a workshop that delves into the mysteries of other fluffy cultures, such as Rabbit, Hamster and Guinea Pig.

5. INTRODUCE A SUGGESTION BOX: This works well for humans, but can be bewildering for cats, who naturally try to climb inside. Also, fluffy staff tend to confuse it with a litterbox, with calamitous results.

INCREASE PRODUCTIVITY

"Productivity is being able
to get humans to do things you were
never able to get them to do before."
FRANZ CATKA

Happy staff are productive staff. Happy staff can't wait to come to work each day and that's just how it is at Office Cat Inc. The human staff can't wait to get to the office to see, pat, listen to, feed and generally obey the fluffy meownagement, and it goes without saying that the feline staff are more than satisfied with this state of affairs. Here are a few of my other top tips for productivity:

1. WORK FROM HOME: Or even better, work from bed, basket or hammock. My favourite place to work is my private island, Catuai, when possible. With today's technology it's easy to delegate remotely.

2. AVOID MICRO-MANAGING: Luckily cats are not micro-managers by nature and are happy to nap on while the

humans complete the menial tasks associated with setting up, running and growing business.

3. SET REALISTIC GOALS: This is important but of course goals are different for cats and humans. I require that the humans keep the business moving forward and that fluffy meownagement get 18 hours of sleep a day.

4. AVOID JOB MONOTONY: As I've previously mentioned, we like to rotate staff now and again so everyone has a chance to try their paw at every job. I have to use my discretion, however, as roof- and tree-top surveillance doesn't seem to suit the humans.

5. WORK OUT: Raise staff fitness levels. All staff members are encouraged to carry out at least one daily 20-minute cardio session of cushion-kneading.

6. INCENTIVE SCHEMES: I recently introduced the Empty Box Bonus where, if a staff member sells a carton of product, they get to keep the empty carton. This has had mixed results, as the humans are nonplussed by this offer and some fluffy staff members are keen to get into and remain in the box to the detriment of their productivity.

STAFF AWARDS AND CELEBRATIONS

"The cat who remembers to thank his
helpers will reap the rewards behind
the ears and under the chin."

ANCIENT PERSIAN PROVERB

As work colleagues often spend more time together than they
do with their own families, it's important to maintain a
friendly atmosphere. And the way to do this is to organise
social occasions where staff can mingle and bond.

At Office Cat Inc. we like
to hold as many social events
as possible. Every Friday
night we have a sardine
sizzle, which all staff are
encouraged to attend as it

I don't mind playing the fool and am the first
one to don the bunny or reindeer ears and
kick off the dog impressions.

allows one final chance for the humans to pat me before the weekend.

I am somewhat of a gourmand and I like to test out my recipes at staff parties. I know the staff thoroughly appreciate me feeding them for a change (of course the actual cooking is done by one of the human staff). I love to surprise my staff with my culinary innovations. Inspurred by the popular butterfly cake, I developed my own variation - the moth cake. Who can resist the light and subtle flavour of moth?

The Annual Giant Trout Award is given to the human member of staff who has shown the strongest improvement in freshwater fishing.

At the end-of-year Christmas party we always have a special awards ceremony. We divide them into Human Support Staff awards and Fluffy Meownagement awards.

HUMAN SUPPORT STAFF AWARDS
- Most litterboxes emptied
- Fastest shrimp-shelling
- Award for innovation in can-opening techniques

FLUFFY MEOWNAGEMENT STAFF AWARDS
- Longest continual nap
- Award for innovation in sleep position
- The Cheshire Cat award for the highest number of mysterious disappearances

A FEW FINAL WISE WORDS...

"Energy and purrsistence conquer all
things - even that pesky red laser dot."

BENJAMIN FANGKLIN

I am a very spiritual cat. As you know,
I don't like to boast, but one of my
nicknames is 'Yoda'.

And so, there you have it.
I hope that the advice and
stories in this book have
helped any prospective mog-
nates get into my mindset and
understand just what it takes
to get to the top and stay
there. Of course, I have
mostly been addressing other
business felines, as it is
they who I feel really have
what it takes to get ahead.
But I hope that my human
readers learned some useful
lessons too.

If you're a human, the best advice I can give you is to continue to know your place and be happy there. It's best that you understand now that you will never be on the same level as cats; sadly you just don't have the same intelligence or abilities, so a supporting role is what you should aspire to and be satisfied with. Put your heart and soul into it - work that litterbox scooper with a smile on your face, take those cat massage and brushing courses in your own time and please, please keep practising and improving your can-opening and shrimp-shelling skills.

For all you business cats out there, it's important to have a vision for the future. And always think big. Don't worry about how many cans of fish there are left in the cupboard; invest in your own fish farm. Don't be disheartened when you reach the bottom of a dried treats packet; set up your own dehydration plant. Don't wait for Christmas to be able to climb into some empty boxes; build a box-making factory. And remember, there are seven billion humans out there ready to help you make your dreams become a reality. All you have to do is fluff out your tail, roll over, look adorable and meow. Goodbye and good luck.

FURRWARD TO THE
FUTURE!

QUIZ

ARE YOU DESTINED FOR GREATNESS?

1. **HOW MANY SHRIMP IS ENOUGH?**

   A) Enough to satisfy my current appetite

   B) Enough to gorge on now and leave some for later

   C) So many I end up throwing up

   D) I don't understand the question

2. **WHAT IS YOUR ULTIMATE DREAM?**

   A) A bowl of shrimp

   B) A crate of shrimp

   C) A year-long holiday on a shrimp trawler

   D) My own shrimp trawler

3. **HOW MUCH SLEEP DO YOU GET ON AN HOURLY BASIS?**

   A) 5–10 minutes

   B) 20–30 minutes

   C) 40–50 minutes

   D) 60 minutes

4. **WHAT IS YOUR ATTITUDE TO OTHER CATS?**

   A) Friendly and cordial at all times

   B) I tolerate their presence as long as they don't steal my food

   C) I chase them off my territory

   D) I befriend the best but trust no-one

5. **WHAT IS YOUR ATTITUDE TO HUMANS?**

   A) I love and respect them

   B) I tolerate their presence as long as they don't steal my food

   C) I have little to no respect for them

   D) They exist only to do my bidding

6. **IF YOU ARE OFFERED A DISH OF FOOD BY YOUR HUMAN STAFF THAT YOU DON'T LIKE, HOW DO YOU REACT?**

   A) I don't like to make waves so I eat it – I'm usually hungry

   B) I immediately run off

   C) I nibble at it but then sulk in the corner looking at my chef ruefully

   D) I refuse to go near it and death-stare the chef until he or she makes me something else

7. **IF YOU FEEL YOU ARE BEING IGNORED BY YOUR HUMAN STAFF, WHAT DO YOU DO?**

   A) Just go to sleep and don't worry about it

   B) Try a few meows but then give up and go to sleep

   C) Start destroying a couch

   D) Roll around on the floor and try a new adorable pose

8. IF SOMEONE TELLS YOU 'NO', WHAT DO YOU DO?

    A) Immediately capitulate

    B) Eventually give in after a couple of hours of being difficult

    C) Use my cutes to get my way

    D) I don't understand the question

9. THE KITTY LITTER SUPPLY HAS RUN OUT AND YOUR TRAY IS EMPTY. WHAT DO YOU DO?

    A) Cross my legs and wait until my human staff get new litter

    B) Go over the fence to the neighbour's house and relieve myself there

    C) Make a noisy nuisance of myself until the staff fix the situation

    D) Relieve myself in the middle of the staffroom floor

10. YOUR HUMAN STAFF WANT TO DRESS YOU UP IN A STUPID OUTFIT FOR HALLOWEEN. WHAT DO YOU DO?

    A) Grin and bear it

    B) Let them put it on me and put up with it for half an hour, then start to meow

    C) Run up the nearest tree and refuse to come down until Halloween is over

    D) Claw the outfit to shreds so the situation is never repeated

IT'S TIME TO ADD UP YOUR SCORES

POINTS	HOW YOU RATE: A = 1, B = 2, C = 3 AND D = 4
10–15	Terrible. You need to take a good look at yourself, my friend. Are you sure you're not a dog?
15–25	Reasonable. You have some good ideas but are destined for a life of mediocrity if you don't pull your furry socks up.
25–35	Pretty good. You seem to be on the right track, but could still improve. A few more focused power naps and you're there.
35–40	Unbelievable. I couldn't have done better myself. Maybe we're related? I see a future full of overflowing bowls of shrimp. Call me.

OTHER BOOKS BY OFFICE CAT

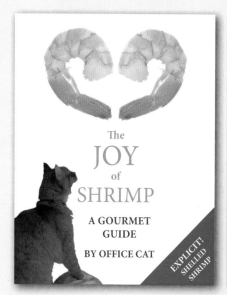

CATKNOWLEDGEMENTS

I would like to dedicate this book to my big sister,
Josie, as well as my personal staff, the Pretty Lady and
Food Clown, who have the honour of looking after my day-
to-day needs. Also, I would like to thank my other beloved
family, the Mooneys (Shaun, Courtney, Archer and Marlowe)
– I would not be where I am today without them. I would
also like to thank my extended family: Lou, Brenda, Mal,
Beverley, Neville, Amanda, Michael, Tim, Jan, Sophie,
Margaret, Puss Whiskin, Serge, Serena, Mehernaz, Marty,
Jeanne, Owen, Seamus and Scoop Ellem.

I would like to thank my publisher, Paul McNally of Smith
Street Books, a long-time fan who repeatedly begged me to
share my business secrets with the world – clearly another
great visionary. I would also like to thank Heather
Menzies and Studio Ginger for their design and Megan Ellis
for her excellent Photoshop 'nip and tuck' skills. Rachel
Day was a wonderful sounding board for ideas and ensured
the essence of my business philosophy wasn't watered down
for the masses.

Thanks to the following for my wardrobe: Amelia Dalton,
BunnyCollarHouse etsy store, ClosLine etsy store and
dharf.com. Thanks also to the Proxy's agent, Fuzz Yard.
When my staff are travelling, I choose to stay at Divine
Creatures, Willoughby, New South Wales, Australia.

PUBLISHED IN 2016 BY SMITH STREET BOOKS
MELBOURNE | AUSTRALIA
SMITHSTREETBOOKS.COM

ISBN: 978-1-925418-12-5

PUBLISHER: PAUL MCNALLY
EDITOR: RACHEL DAY
DESIGN CONCEPT: HEATHER MENZIES, STUDIO31 GRAPHICS
DESIGN LAYOUT: STUDIO GINGER
PREPRESS & IMAGE WORK: MEGAN ELLIS
TALENT: OFFICE CAT

PRINTED & BOUND IN CHINA BY C&C OFFSET PRINTING CO., LTD.

BOOK 11
10 9 8 7 6 5 4 3 2 1

PICTURE CREDITS: ALL PHOTOGRAPHS BY ARIANA KLEPAC AND PETE SMITH EXCEPT FOR THE FOLOWING:
ISTOCK: 6, 61 TOP LEFT, 89 BOTTOM
SHUTTERSTOCK: 1, 8, 16, 19, 20–1, 28, 31, 32–3, 35, 44, 45, 47, 48, 49, 50, 51, 52, 53, 57, 59, 66, 67, 71, 73, 74, 75, 76–7, 80, 84 TOP,
92, 95 TOP, 96–7, 101, 103, 110 (SHRIMP, SARDINES, SARDINE CAN)